You, Love, and the Universe

Patrick Anthony Ramsey

ISBN: 0692851860

ISBN 13: 9780692851869

Chapter One

The Call to Love

When did this journey into the physical world all begin? The Church of Light (www.light.org), and this is also a journey in itself—twenty-one courses, actually, teaches there are ten realms in the cycle of necessity through which each soul, including your soul, passes: celestial, spiritual, astral, mineral, vegetable, animal, human, astral, spiritual, and back once again to celestial.

To this day, I wake up in the day or in the night in these embraces of heartfelt, personal, and passionate interactions with the Universe, which I call it, in short, "The call to love and be loved." I wake up to once again review various written works that we have been working on (the Universe and I), often with greater depth, and with only an occasional rewrite or so, and yes, I promise, there will be further revisions yet to come. This endeavor is the on-going embrace of unending love, affection, comfort, joy, oneness, support, and oh yes, all that is, was, or will ever be a recurring theme! In these special moments of my life, I embrace these energies that give hope, strength, and love to the Universe and both warm and strengthen my human heart.

When in the future, I am physically dead and there is nothing more on this physical plane, moving on to the astral, the only thing left to say would be, "I have in the past, I do in the present, and I shall always in the future love you with the greatest of depth that I can possibly possess!" In short, may these heartfelt stories create in you a burning desire to share, embrace, and celebrate yourselves toward the greatest endeavors yet to come for you to accomplish in your human lives.

Chapter Two

The Story of Missy, the Piscean Cat

Today, we would ask you to hold your healing intentions for those whom you care most about, normally vocalized in our daily healing service, close to your heart. (The Church of Light has a daily healing service, which is said every day at noon for the intentions of its members and loved ones.) We would also ask that you hold yourself there in this healing place along with all that you hold dear. In this service, we are going to try to create enough energy to unite with advanced souls on the inner plane for the purpose of healing our requests, ourselves, and our loved ones body, mind, and soul with some white magic.

I am going to share with you today a story about the evolution of the soul. When you have pets, such as cats and dogs, you take care of them, feed them, and clean up after them. Often your pets destroy things. It is not always a pleasant experience. But when your pet chooses to love you in return, then the experiences that follow are unique, special, and transformational. These experiences provide a wealth of give-and-take, which results in both souls developing spiritually in the interactions, becoming better than they previously were. It becomes obvious over time that each soul is one with the Universe. Each soul is indeed a spiritual being and an emanation of powers of goodness and kindness, often with a little kick.

I first met Missy the cat while dropping off Christmas gifts at Phyllis Pohler's house one Christmas Eve with my wife, Radine; perhaps it was in our ninth or tenth year of marriage, not sure. Radine's grandmother, Peggy, who is in her nineties, was there. As we sat in Phyllis's living room,

I on a chair and Radine on the couch, Phyllis's two cats, Rosie and Missy, were also there. Missy was a long-haired black cat with green eyes. Rosie was a gray cat with black stripes. There we were, when Missy decided to jump in my lap. Peggy and Phyllis looked at each other aghast, anticipating what might happen next. As Missy got comfortable on my lap, a few moments later Rosie decided to come near. Missy started hissing at Rosie, like a snake warning its prey. Missy turned out to be very possessive of the people she liked and objected to any other cat trying to interfere. Yes, well, I had some scratches on my legs that day!

One day into the summer that same year, on a Sunday at the beginning of August, we prepared a large meal at our Burbank home to celebrate Peggy's birthday, a Leo. Peggy and Phyllis, Radine's father, Ray Hayes, his wife Melanie, Ray's son Michael and Melanie's daughter Katie were all present for our celebration. We prepared a nice meal and ate on a large table on our back patio. The weather was pleasant and we ate early enough that you could still feel the cool morning air.

Unfortunately, it became obvious that Phyllis was not well, but was not completely aware of it. However, she enjoyed the meal and the company. She had lost quite a bit of weight, but surprisingly, she did not realize she was ill. Not too long after that, she was diagnosed with advanced colon cancer. She passed away in the hospital and was cremated, as per her wishes. Radine and I were asked to take her cats.

In the Church of Light, we teach the evolution of the soul that advances through a series of incarnations from mineral to plant to animal to human. We can spiritually talk with plants and trees, and in doing so, this is one glimpse we can have into our evolving process. Our pets often provide a greater glimpse into our own souls through our daily interactions, reminding us that we were perhaps once someone's pet in times long gone by.

Where are your moment-to-moment experiences stored? Are they stored in your mind? Some of them are stored there for a short time. There are some things that you will always remember, but there are some things you will not. The detailed moment–to-moment experiences are stored in our individual souls, which one day in the future we can recall. These are the experiences that are reviewed at the end of life during the assimilation process, a preparation toward something greater yet to come.

Where do thoughts exist? Some thoughts exist in the mind. Most thoughts happen at a rate faster than the speed of light. From our teachings, we know if something is faster than the speed of light, then it exists on the astral and spiritual planes. Thoughts then existing on the astral and spiritual planes, given enough thought energy and given the proper ingredients and circumstances present in the physical world, can manifest into our physical environment. That is why it is so important, moment to moment, to take care what thoughts you entertain in your consciousness. I guess what I am saying is to be mindful of your thoughts in that what you think can manifest into the physical plane. In short, ask yourself, is what you think what you really want?

Have you ever been talking with someone and suddenly you could not remember something? And you say, "Wait a minute, it will come to me." You go on with what you were doing and let it go, and then, at some time in the near future, what eluded you suddenly pops into your mind. And you say, "Ah-ha! Now I remember." This is merely an example of directed thinking and extending your consciousness to your soul, obtaining the information you seek, and then bringing it back into the physical plane, your reality.

The real you is your soul, and it already exists on the astral and spiritual planes. You are physically here, but one day, as will happen to all of us, our physical body will eventually wear out and we will return to existing only as a spiritual being. Your soul grows through daily experiences. You want a wealth of experiences so that your soul is well rounded; another way of saying it is that it is vastly important to embrace the loves of your life and all those who are present to you so that through these physical experiences you grow spiritually.

How do spiritual experiences happen in our daily lives? Very often, I will be going about my daily activities and then suddenly some other soul pops into my consciousness. Sometimes, but not always, it is someone who has passed away and is on the inner plane. Sometimes that happens when I am shaving in the morning. Now is the soul who has popped into my consciousness in the same physical room as I am? I don't think so, at least I hope not! More likely this is a soul who has a question or needs to resolve a matter with me and who has tuned into my soul on the astral and spiritual planes. The matter or question pops into my mind as I shave, and I respond and answer this question on a spiritual level by responding directly to this soul in loving ways. Once I respond, the matter usually resolves. I wish them well and off they go. The point is there is a resolution of something that was unfinished, usually resolving something that was troubling this other soul.

As long as you are on a high spiritual plane, those who tune into you must raise their consciousness to that level in order to communicate with you. It is true you can tune your consciousness into any level, but it is not always wise to do so, especially if it is a lower level.

A few years ago, Neil Cantwell, a Hermetican in the Church of Light, spoke about extending your consciousness to solve crimes, but also that it was not recommended, as you are tuning into another consciousness, which is not healthy. Crimes, however, can be solved in that way. A far better way is to ask a spiritual question, for which you do not have the answer, to your soul already on the inner planes, which in turn seeks the various answers to your questions, and then conveys the information that later comes back into your physical consciousness to resolve your question. Many acts of injustice are not solved on this plane of consciousness, but rest assured, what is not resolved on the physical plane will necessarily be resolved on the astral and spiritual planes. Some resolutions ultimately take some time to work out and resolve, but one day resolved they will all be. Why is that? It is because we must all, one day, stand together in love and kindness, forgiving and learning from one another in order to move forward to create greater acts of love and kindness in future endeavors.

Now back to Missy. Phyllis had just passed on to the inner plane, and there came Pat and Radine to her apartment to collect Rosie and Missy.

Radine said I should have worn gloves, and she was right! We brought two cat carriers. Rosie was easy, but Missy did not want to go. She finally darted into the bedroom and under the bed. We went in there with our cat carrier and closed the door. I had to pick-up the bed to get to her. She scratched my hand pretty good, but the deed was done.

We did receive Missy's medical records from Peggy. The first thing we noticed in her records were the words stamped, "Caution, will bite."

After a couple of weeks, Rosie and Missy, both females, adjusted to our all-male cat environment there in our home in Burbank, California. It was not too long before the two female cats were running the show, with an occasional male objection.

One day, I am not sure exactly when, Missy decided I was hers. I was busy working on the home computer. She would unexpectedly jump into my lap as if to say, "You are going to stop working and pay attention to me." In retrospect, I always get interrupted while working on my computer. I now consider it part of a normal daily routine because it is what the external consciousness of pets and others is proclaiming, "What you are doing there is trivial, but I am more important and you must pay attention to me." I would have to stop everything and hold Missy. If another cat would come too near, she again would hiss, but she would finally stop scratching me, and yes, the danger was always there.

In August of 2006, we decided to sell our home in Burbank and move here to Albuquerque, New Mexico, the present headquarters of the Church of Light. In the last week of 2006, we made our way here with two cars filled with our cats and rabbits. We arrived here after a record local snowstorm with three large PODS of belongings to follow in January.

Shortly after we moved here, Missy was diagnosed with a two-inch inoperable mass in her abdomen. How did this happen? It is difficult to say. We each occupy different environments. Unfortunately, something had already manifested in Missy, which would eventually take her life. We made her as comfortable as possible. She continued finding me working at my desk on the computer and wanting to be held frequently, which I did.

She would defiantly stand on the top of our rollaway files for Pat Aeronautics, Inc., then new and pristine files. At that time, it was our vendor file. She would eat, and then twenty minutes or so later, she would be on the files and begin heaving. Barfing would scare Missy. She would do a running barf, spreading her contents over our files. I would come running across the room, yelling, "No!" It was mostly too late! While Missy recovered somewhere else in the house and secluded, I would slowly clean the files with moist paper towels, never to be pristine again!

Normally, when a pet can no longer eat and the quality of life seems to have disappeared, the animal doctor does the humane thing. In Missy's case, she was still eating and fighting to hang on. To her dying day, she still mustered the strength to jump on my desk, wanting to be held. That day she was quite thin. I spread some bath towels on my waterbed and carried her in and laid her down. I looked into her green eyes and said, "You are quite a soul, Missy! It's OK to move on to something better. I am sure Phyllis will be there to greet you. I love you, Missy, and I will always hold a place for you in my heart." That evening, I returned to my waterbed and she had moved on. We enter this world through a doorway of pain and suffering and we take our leave through that same doorway, with the next life promising to be better.

The other day, now a few years later, I came across this file folder of one of the vendors, Aircomponents West. Yes, indeed, there it was; it was Missy barf! Missy has been gone a few years now, but even Missy barf is now special. Some would have thrown this folder in the trash. But now, having Missy gone, to me it has unlimited value, a reminder of the power of unending and limitless love.

We need these types of stories to heal ourselves and others, to evoke in us an emotion for healing purposes and also emotional releases. From an eternal viewpoint, wouldn't it be interesting, years from now, to look into the next human incarnation for Missy or your own pet? I would say this: I am her advocate!

Oh, thou Eternal Spirit in whom we live, move, breathe, and have our being, we invite you into our lives for direction and healing. We call upon the angelic community and all advanced souls who work on the astral and spiritual planes to heal us, body, mind, and soul. Evoking the universal law, as above, so below, may these healing energies find paths to manifest into our spiritual temple, our physical body, our peace of mind, and our wholeness of being.

What are your unique and special gifts you are born with to make our earth a better place and both strengthen and heal the souls you daily encounter? Do you know your best planet for making money? (You would need your natal birth chart for this: date, time, and place of birth, along with the source of this data for accuracy purposes. If any of the birth data is not accurate, then the natal chart is not accurate either. The birth chart is the unique map of the soul, all the experiences the soul has had up to that moment of birth. Volumes can be written on any single birth chart.) Ideally, your best planet for making a living is the same as what you are supposed to be doing toward making our earth a better place, but often they are not the same, and each of us, in our own way, have to work on two separate paths—one to make a living and eat and another to change the earth through the blessings of our own uniqueness, but what such a sacred path each soul's journey truly is!

We teach that with angelic blessing the soul divides into two monads, male and female, and begins its journey through a series of incarnations through mineral, plant, animal, man, and then the male and female soul mates eventually reunite in the spiritual plane. The separate experiences by both the male and female earthly incarnation are assimilated and reviewed in the soul between each incarnation. So why do you think it is that we don't run into our soul mate on this planet? Of course, sometimes we do and may not even know it. It is better for each soul to experience a wealth of different experiences so that when the two monads do eventually reunite there is a greater realization, something that the Universe can use to create in both of you something of greater value. It is my feeling too that these incarnations may perhaps occur on more than one planet.

Let us endeavor to heal and now strengthen one another. Oh, thou Eternal Spirit in whom we live, move, breathe, and have our being, we invite you into our beings for direction and healing.

May all that is whole and centered bring you happiness, usefulness, and physical and spiritual well-being so that you are more on purpose to realize success in all areas of your life.

May goodness, kindness, and positive spirituality help create in you tolerance, patience, and acceptance along with healing, enduring, and empowering love.

One day when you move from this world into the next life, as we all one day will, may you realize how much you are loved.

So it shall be, and so it is.

Chapter Three

Let's Talk about the Transformation of Moving Mountains

Take it from a Scorpion, no one can love you like the Universe. It is better than sex, but of course, when the Universe loves you through someone else, that is something exceedingly special.

The love of the Universe is such that it does not know Catholic, Jewish, Muslim, but feels its way across the earth seeking the human soul to heal it and bring it back into oneness with all that is, was, or will ever be. The Universe does not see walls or borders, but only souls, developing, evolving toward something greater.

Today's Scorpion sermon is about the transformation of moving mountains. Growing up in Burbank, California, we were surrounded by mountains. My Capricorn mom and I used to go to the 12:15 p.m. Mass every Sunday at St. Finbar; I grew up with a heavy Catholic foundation. I remember one scripture talked about commanding a mountain to get up and move over there and it would. I was looking at the mountain there in Burbank, and I said, well, if you ask this mountain to get up and move over there, all the people living on that mountain are not going to be too happy! And what is more, wherever the mountain moves to, those people living there are going to be a little pissed too! Well, I put this to the Universe, and of course, there was no answer at that time. The Universe probably thought, "Stupid kid!"

I graduated from John Burroughs Senior High School, class of 1994. I used to sit around during lunch with the same friends. Each year, we had the Akela yearbooks, our yearly high school annual in which some of your classmates wrote personal things to you at the end of the year. As in most yearbooks, your classmates would write various words in it, some good, some not so good! From my 1972 yearbook from Roger Carroll:

> "Patrick—You've got 2 years but I've got 1, so stick with it
> kid and have a nice Summer. Se ya, maybe Roger Caroll
> P.S. Try not to argue with Ken and Compton too much.

What we used to argue about sometimes during lunch was whether it was OK to be gay or not. I had grown up a Catholic and because of this influence, I argued that it was not, but not having the wisdom at that time to realize that those I was arguing with were so inclined. When you are young, you are really stupid and do not realize it. You are ignorant of the true feelings of others. Since then, today I have come to the conclusion that is it not so much who you love, but rather that you love. Years later, I now realize that if you were to remove gay or straight from your mind-set entirely, it would be easy to conclude that there is only love. This expression of love, wherever it might take you, is a heathy growth process toward building healthy and happy relationships and should be given the freedom to grow without judgment or condemnation. By accepting who you are today, you empower and strengthen your personal growth process. What you start out as today may and often does change over time. Therefore, give yourself the freedom to change.

That summer, Roger did call me at home, but I was not too much allowed out of the house, and I am not sure how he got my number. I was seventeen at the time. I had my paper route and my home chores and, besides TV, not too much more. I do not know the circumstances, but that summer it became too much for Roger to go on. I did not know the exact details. In reality, I did not even know where he lived or even how to contact his family or what his family was like. What I learned later from another classmate passing me in the school hall was that Roger somehow swallowed Alcester and then followed it up with a glass of water. He passed away from a burst stomach ulcer, internal bleeding.

To anyone, death seems so final at the time it happens, an abrupt separation. There are probably people in all of our lives for whom if we could we would move back the clock and do or say some things differently, and if we could, we should, but we can't. And there are souls, people that we will never forget, of whom we always have memories and hold each of them dear to our hearts. Often, after a time, I do have experiences of people who have passed on popping into my life for a moment to communicate in some way or make an attempt to try to resolve something. Of those who have committed suicide, until earlier this year, I have not had any contact. Earlier this year, I did feel Roger; we apparently had some like vibrations and similar feelings. He is OK and his soul continues to progress on the inner plane, and we continue to communicate every once in a while. Death is not so permanent a separation as at first you might conclude! But it does take some time, varying with each person, for the soul to assimilate on the inner astral plane. The soul is assimilating all the past experiences of various incarnations in preparation for something greater. I would say this too, love knows no bounds. And that's important because love does reach out beyond the grave and speaks truth and gives both support and strength to the human soul. Good and true heartfelt thoughts, feelings, and the transformational powers of goodness, kindness, and love do necessarily heal on all levels of being.

In my opinion, those who have passed away due to suicide are wounded souls, who for whatever reason found it too difficult to continue to live on this physical plane. It takes longer for these souls to assimilate on the inner plane and move forward, but as we teach in the Church of Light, no soul is ever lost and will continue to advance. I would say too that when our love reaches out to various souls and is freely and genuinely given it has the transformational power to heal various wounds of the past. It is this transformational power that frees the wounded soul to move on toward greater endeavors.

The Universe is such that if one soul needs help the Universe sends out the troops to support that person. Take a hard look at this planet; there are certainly many souls who have lost their way and need direction and help. That is why so many of us are here in this present life. If you were to consider mental illnesses alone on this planet, it is overwhelming. It is obvious that we need to spend more resources in helping others, teaching parenting, and helping others to address anger management issues in their lives and that is an understatement!

Our twenty-one courses in the Church of Light can and does help souls find direction and strength. Our courses are transformational and make this world a better place. We have something unique that we should encourage others to read and make their lives better than it might otherwise be.

Let us now together move into a meditative state. In your own way, move into your own private meditative place. Be open to accept blessings from the Universe.

"You have provided to others encouragement and strength of nature where there was only sorrow and depression."

"You have provided direction and hope to people in confinement, who have made mistakes and lost their way."

"You provided ways toward enlightenment to souls with steadfast positions who when presented with other paths have changed their hearts and now contribute in better ways."

"You in your persistence, strength, and unceasing work have paved ways for others to take their rightful place in the Universe contributing in unique ways, like no one else can, advancing the Universe forward in our world today."

"And so says the Universe to your soul, what is more, don't you know, "You have moved mountains, after all!"

Remember, then, sons and daughters of the earth, that nothing can resist a firm will, which has for a lever the knowledge of the true and just. To combat in order to secure its realization is more than right; it is a duty. Those who triumph in that struggle accomplish their earthly mission; those who succumb by devoting themselves to it gain immortality. If the sovereign (Scorpio) should appear in the prophetic signs of your horoscope, it signifies that the realization of your hopes depends upon a being more powerful than yourself. Seek to know the Universe and the Universe will have your back at times when you most need it. So shall it be, and so it is!

Chapter Four

The Evolution of the Soul is a Wondrous and Glorious Thing

When walking our dog, Elsa, there is something transcendent, magical, a new unrepeated adventure into the cosmos. The walk, something longed for forever it would seem, is special, unique, a once in a lifetime experience, never to be the same ever again. This is a journey of love and expectation. It is winter, but the sun is shining, and although the breeze is cold, its rays are warm. We walk along the path, now dry; the irrigation stopped during winter. But there are still the horses and cows, glad of our presence. We still pass by two very old trees with such large trunks that I pause and place my hand on the trunk. The trunks are cold and very dry, but there is a presence within the tree that is glad to have this touch. These trees are deserving of so much more—cultivation, weeding, minerals, pruning, adornment with flowers, perhaps in the hope that spring would follow. For now, Ms. Dog, Elsa, is content in rolling in the dirt of autumn past.

We look at the Sandias, the mountains of New Mexico in the Western morning light, and I hear a single voice, a higher pitch above the movement of everyday life, and I say to myself, "This is one of the many blessings of the Universe to the souls of the earth," as if higher beings are present, watching our every move, hoping of greater things to come.

One day, when I pass away from this earth, one of the first things I would like to do, if I can, is look into the future lives of our pets to see how they are doing in their human incarnations. And if I could, I would be their advocate! Why would that be, you ask; it is because I love them so. I desire that they more than make their way, but advance this earth forward in spiritual and physical ways, that one day when they too pass into the inner plane I may be given the grace and blessings to embrace their souls and say in my most heartfelt way, "I love you." And be honest, have we not all felt that way about our pets? Have you not felt that way about your children in this life?

Controversial, you say, because a dog or cat is not like a person. Are you so very sure? Ultimately, we must rise above our daily existence and embrace a Higher Power. It is a pause in time when the Universe quietly looking on at us also pauses. The music wells up and creates in us gladness, joy, wonderment, thanksgiving, and all the joys of oneness because of our great love together. One day, a dog or cat will evolve into human form, just as you will move forth from this earth to evolve into greater existence.

We teach in our Church of Light courses that the cycle of necessity through which the soul passes is celestial, spiritual, astral, mineral, vegetable, animal, human, astral, spiritual, and then once again back to celestial. These are the various paths of the Universe for each of you, the various paths your lives take; perhaps think of it as an adventure! The Universe plots, plans, and schemes, just as many of us do every day, in silence on your behalf to find better ways for your soul to advance and arrive at a better understanding toward your various paths of enlightenment. Don't scold us so much, if we make a mistake, but realize it was a mistake on your behalf. We can never underestimate how much we truly love and care for each other or how much the Universe takes unseen action toward these endeavors beyond our present awareness, but make no mistake, one day, all of this we will know for each of us!

That brings us to Gilligan, the Aries cat! He is gray and black, close to an Egyptian Mau, but not quite so, but always close enough for me! Gilligan is full of piss and vinegar. He was so named because as a kitten he climbed up our pine tree in the backyard of our Burbank home and then climbed to the end of the branch. As he dangled from the end of a pine tree branch in his exuberance, about twelve feet in the air, there was I beneath him, bracing to catch him in his fall. When he fell, I partially caught him, but he fell on his tail. His tail was slightly bent for the rest of his life, but from that moment on, he became and will always be Gilligan, my little buddy.

When we moved from Burbank to Albuquerque in 2006 and started Pat Aeronautics out of our home, we started purchasing black letter-size filing cabinets all in a row to house our paperwork that we needed to hold for seven years, per state department requirements. Well, here comes Gilligan, in his universal statement of sorts, to christen these filing cabinets with his tail raised and urine spraying! Of course, as I was eating breakfast at the time, I stood up abruptly and said, "You damn cat!" And off he ran as fast as he could, me chasing him, and I, of course, was not able to catch him. Today you can see a slight rust stain on the bottom of our filing cabinets, a stain to some but a blessing in fact in the years to come.

Gilligan would get behind my work chair when I would be at the computer working and meow at the top of his lungs to let him out the door, his way of saying, "Get off your fat ass and let me out." (I was slightly fatter at the time, 218 pounds, and now I am 176 or so!) He would go on a morning walkabout every day in the local area, also anointing with his unique spray along his way, which I did find out later did bother our neighbor, more than I knew at the time. He did this every day so religiously that it was almost like he was walking his dog, Spot. I used to kid him that he was walking his dog, prior to going to work at his local law firm of Gilligan, Gilligan, and Gilligane! But when he was done with his walk, he would stand outside our closed door and meow at the top of his lungs; his way of saying, "Get off your fat ass and let me in."

Gilligan would affectionately lick my arm on occasion and cleaned me in his own unique way, a continual healing event—in retrospect, his way of saying, "I love you, and yes, you taste good." There were also times I would find him on my waterbed, licking himself where most people can't, but at the end of the day, so what? (To be honest, I know quite a few people who wished they could lick themselves there, but as growth and interacting with others goes, that is probably why cats and dogs are different: humans need to interact with one another for reasons of higher purposes.)

As is in the Aries nature, Gilligan was a fighter. He would persist in his vocal meowing so much so that some days, in an effort to quiet him, we would place him in a bedroom by himself, on a bed alone, and close the door. Of course, ten minutes later, Gilligan would be sound asleep and snoring. Aries does fight, but in reality, becomes exhausted from that endeavor. But really, nothing looks so pure and innocent as a soul peacefully sleeping.

Gilligan unexpected and quickly in early December 2010 developed a fast-growing carcinoma of the mouth, not sure how or why. Radine and I were in denial at first, but in reality, he fast became a cat that could not eat or function. On the night before, I took him into my arms and said, "I shall always love you. There has never been a soul with so much energy and function that I have known and I shall never forget you, always love you, always wish you good fortune in your future endeavors and I shall always hold you close to my heart."

How does Gilligan, an Aries cat, fit into a Cancer service? In a real way, there are windows in our physical lives, special moments, events that follow us around forever, a Higher Power moving with and about us. Aries in reality is not that far apart from Cancer, when you consider this matter of love. It creeps up on us, and when we turn around to see this love, it darts always, sideways out of our sight, but we know it is still there because we can feel it. Rising above it all, if we were to sit down and silently long for this love to return, would it suddenly dart back into our life just as rapidly in order to feel the love and joy of our existence? Personally, I think so!

At the end of our days, you want the Universe to be able to look into your eyes and say, "If I could have anyone to protect my back, it would be you." In the end, the Cosmic Mind communicates uniquely to you in special, miraculous ways, a special blessing and fellowship for your soul—to empower your wholeness, support your uniqueness, and confirm in you your wellness of being, your unique gifts to help everyone.

Remember then, sons and daughters of the earth, that whosoever braves the unknown does so at his or her own peril. Hostile minds, figured by the black dog, will surround you with ambushes; servile minds will offer you flatteries; and treacherous minds, like unto the Scorpion, will plan your ruin. If Arcanum 18 should appear in the prophetic signs of your horoscope, observe and listen, but know how to be silent, for in your silence the Universe will assist you and heal you amid your varied paths, but know that I shall always love you and hold you close to my loving heart today, tomorrow, and forever.

For more information on the Major Arcanum, please refer to Course 6, The Sacred Tarot, of the Church of Light: www.light.org

From Course 18, Imponderable Forces:

17. What are the three essential functions of ceremonial magic?

(1) *Arousing emotions to furnish the magical purposes.*
(2) *To contact those on the inner plane to assist.*
(3) *To direct energy to the right channel.*

We try to create magic in our lives, but in retrospect, we do not always see the magic that is already in and surrounding our lives; we do not fully appreciate it, except when we are reminded. So here I am to remind you of how blessed you really are.

Join with me. Pray with me. Be with me as we touch with our hands the physical air around us in our present environment, the presence of the Universe. The air throbs and pulses, but also to me, what we touch is and will ever be the Universal Being, desiring so much to experience with each of us our physical life. I believe that it is the presence of the Universal Mind that makes the physical dimension even possible at all. This physical environment that you move within every day is the physical energy of the Universe. What you touch, what you feel, what you sense with your hands is the presence of a higher desire to advance your lives and the lives around you to make our world a better place, both now and into our future.

I decided to omit the ceremonial magic part of this ceremony from this work because you have to experience it in person. It is unique and special to you. Angels are involved, as well as your ancestry and many healing souls. I tried to find ways to convey it numerous times, but unsuccessfully. We are going to attempt this anyway, but perhaps we can come together in the future sometime meeting as a crowd to create something greater:

We call forth our vast and deep emotions from within us: Our emotions are our profound love for others in our daily lives, who are around us and who touch our hearts in so many ways, even if we do not admit it. Some may be sick in some way. Some have already passed on to the next life. Some have disappeared seemingly, permanently from our present life, but are still alive and present somewhere on this earth, we may not know where. Some move within our circle still, but are as distant planets, far away. May our hearts now desire to draw these souls closer for the purposes of healing, oneness, and love. We must personally say to them: treasures of so many souls shall never be buried beneath the sands of distant, faraway islands, but be eternally present within our hearts henceforth, now, and forever.

We call upon all higher-minded souls to add their healing energies to our presence. The angelic community, a strength and saving grace that we seldom see working in our lives, is now here present. We call upon all that is good, whole, centered, loving, and cosmic-minded to add their healing vibrations of wholeness, physical, and spiritual wellness of being calm with a sense of peace and love. May our ministerial efforts together bring healing, peace, and harmony to everyone in our lives.

We now direct these energies toward making our world around us completely whole and healed physically, mentally, and spiritually. May all tears be dried, all hurts be resolved, and all losses be healed. Know this our earth is healed not so much from our great efforts to do so, but from our tremendous love united here together that has indeed already made it so.

Each of us struggles with our lives in ways we will never show others and in some ways never admit to ourselves. Know that the Universe already knows and loves you. Let us rejoice in our love and live together. Listen now and be present to angels singing: a million or so in the base section, a million tenors, a million altos, a million sopranos, and a million or so of various singing sections in between perfected on the inner plane into multiple sections.

Going forward, then listen, not so much to the words, but become a part of such powerful reverberations of love and intent: As we hear a distant sound from a faraway mountain, see the sun slowly rise over the face of the earth to greet the many diverse trees, mountains, valleys, deserts, towns, and waters.

The angels have perfected this piece of art in ways that provide specific healings, directed uniquely to specific individuals who really need it the most:

At some point in the near future, perhaps in a dream, or on being awakened in the middle of your night, you may begin a conversation with the Universe. Do not dismiss it slightly, but be present to it. Enjoy it and participate in it! In this unique conversation, possibly toward its conclusion, at some point listen openly to the possibility of hearing choirs of angels! And if too, unplanned, you fall peacefully asleep due to the blessed sounds that you hear, consider yourself specially blessed.

Hear various choirs singing as the sun sets slowly into the eastern skies amid passing storm clouds of heavy rain, thunder, and lightning. Powerful and ominous it is! Yet be comforted in the strength and trust in the Universe because you know in your heart how much you are loved. As the sun sets in the east, an angel sings a resounding note across the mountains, valleys, and planes, "This is one of the many blessings of the Universe to the souls of the earth."

Chapter Five

The Grace, Blessing, and Empowerment of Being Human

Na Na na na, na-na na na Na-na na na, hey Jude.

I dance with Elsa the golden retriever and sing this; she loves it! Some might say that "Na" is not a word, but in Aries fashion, yes, it is! The Beatles—we have all lived and breathed a part of that, have we not? In the quite cool of the early night, when all have gone to bed and are asleep, the Universe moves across the earth to interact with those souls who are awake. We gather in unity together, most completely unaware of each other, but all saying similar messages:

"We must always guard the sanctity of family love."

That, in my opinion, is the heart and soul as well as the ongoing motive of Aries.

We now call upon all souls who are good, kind, and generous to be in our presence now. The earth is transformed through the power of love. Join with me now, if you are so inclined.

Aries brings such powerful energies. These powerful energies can last and take root into daily earthly actions, when supported by others with the ongoing powers of truth and love. Mars loves like no other, often too intense, but it is always fulfilling. Some of us have seen the *Fifty Shades of Grey*, but more important in fact is the intimacy, something that is the most important thing of all and often ignored or dismissed. Intimacy is greater than the act itself because at the end if you can embrace and hold each other, be at peace and bask in the glow of how much you truly love each other, then congratulations, you are among the most blessed and the luckiest humans on the face of the earth. Such is the empowering and ongoing power of love.

That, of course, brings us to Pepper the cat, Aries, and this time, a story that does not end in death, thankfully! Peeps is sprawled atop his domain of the Konica Minolta Bizhub 222 copier/dual fax/scanner, breathing deeply as he dreams of past conquests, and if you pause, past the reality that he is sleeping on a very expensive piece of equipment that he has claimed as his, you can see the strength, tranquility, and indeed, the beauty of Aries. If the universal mind were to pause here and make any comment, it would be: the love of the Universe is good and it continually, eternally embraces all that is whole and all that is wonderful. Peeps struts his stuff, holds his tail on high, beckons you to touch his beauty, and then bites you for doing so.

The thing to remember about our pets is that one day, perhaps sooner than you might think as centuries go, they will all in the near future embody a human existence. If we are to endeavor to change the future for the better, we must go beyond and empower our pets toward greater good, kindness, truth, and love. Therefore, we must think about our daily interactions with our pets on a daily basis going forward, keeping in mind our pets will one day be human, in the next life. What were you in your previous incarnation, care to gather a guess?

Then there is Elvis the cat who appeared one day at our Burbank home. She was a very feminine and black cat that I at the time thought to myself, "Radine needs to get this cat to Dr. Calic (our vet) fast and get her fixed before she becomes pregnant." Radine took Elvis to Dr. Calic, who looked and said, laughing, "Neutered male, no charge." We were going to give Elvis back to the pet store from where he somehow escaped, only to later realize that he actually belonged with us. We paid the pet store one hundred dollars and kept him. Later, I realized that Elvis had been sexually abused as a kitten; some people should not have pets at all. Elvis loved to be held by Radine, but treated me, a male of my species, as the enemy and still does to this day. Other times, over the years, I observed Elvis humping other male cats, playing dominant kitty to the likes of Gilligan. I can pet Elvis at 2:30 a.m., the feeding time, the only time of the day I can pet him and extend a loving touch, but if I arrive back five minutes later, he will run away.

Elvis loves to open my drawers, such as my waterbed drawers, and with his cat claws throws my underwear and socks high up in the air, which I endeavor to keep neat. He also endeavors to open our kitchen drawer containing our dish towels. Then afterward, along come Peeps, who decided to sleep in the dish towel drawer, very cozy, warm, and comfortable, I'm sure. The little shits! And if that is not enough, Elvis occasionally employees Peeps for his endeavors and opens the kitchen turntable, where Peeps passes afterward with his tail raised, spraying his unique Peeper spray upon our canned goods! And yes, this gives a whole new meaning to the word "Pepper spray."

You have probably all seen pictures of Junior, our little orange cat, in a past Church of Light quarterly (all publications accessed for free at www. light.org) He was fixed too young, but because of that, he is blessed with a perfect soprano, some of the most pure and uplifting sounds that you could ever hear! When I get up around 2:30 a.m., a must now, my purpose at this time has become feeding the cats. There is Junior in the hall, on the way to the kitchen, trying to interact with the hound, another orange cat who thinks he is a Chihuahua, only because he was raised as a kitten with baby Chihuahuas. But here is Junior, now fully grown, but still a small cat, as cats go, literally bouncing off the hall walls and singing for joy in his high-pitched soprano voice in expectation of the celebration of food at 2:30 a.m. And if I were to now try to sleep in past 2:30 a.m., poor me, a cat ruckus would ensue until I reneged—probably about 2:35 a.m. or so. Then there is Squigglie, one of the friendliest and most social cats you would ever meet. He is the most good-natured of our cats. I am not sure of his sun sign, but if I were to try to pinpoint it, it would be the sign of love. But wait, you say that is not a sign, but ultimately, I would beg to differ, because love encompasses all the signs. Each day, I clean and start to prepare four bowls of various Fancy Feast. Gemini, the now elder alpha cat, now only has ten out of thirty teeth—not so easy for him to eat, but he manages.

From my observations, the poignant vulnerability of Aries is in daily family life. Other family members can create death actions for Aries that are often hard and impossible to reverse or overcome during the course of a normal life. In our world, all of us can rightly ask, "What is a normal life?" The Aries solution for this is to not be a victim of death of some sort by a family member, but instead to form another family bond through some other living soul who is more deserving. The assumption here is that Aries, in some way, can find a way to continue and to separate from the acts of others held most dear to find greater good and not be killed by passed events of trusted loved ones. Be assured, there are some life events that can only be resolved on the inner plane after physical death, but resolved they shall be! I applaud those Aries souls who have risen to the occasion and found ways forward. For those who have not found ways forward in this life, I assure you that there will be ways forward in the next life on the inner plane when you arrive there. Even in the direst circumstances, the Universe will always find a way for you to move forward, because such is the power of universal and parental love. Perhaps at the end of this journey, when all are whole again, all tears are dried, maybe then there can begin to be something we night call "normal."

People in our world struggle so constantly to have power. Our teaching indicates correctly that goodness alone is power. We have all seen false power, others who seek to prey and take advantage of others for their own selfish gain. They succeed and call this power, but it is not. It is only a path of destruction and false fulfilment that at some point disappears into nothingness. At the end of life, if all that you have left is love, then indeed, you have succeeded in life beyond all possible measures!

Have you ever noticed that many people who minister to others say the same thing? We all have similar messages, but say it in different ways, from different parts of this earth, but hopefully empowering enlightenment in others, encouraging others toward more positive paths. Today we are going to do a healing experiment. I am going to ask you to touch someone else in a healing way; nothing intimidating, all you need to do is place your hands on someone else's shoulders and whisper the words "I love you" in their ears. Keep in mind that "there's nothing you can do that can't be done." Healings take place because we care for and love one another. There is "nothing you can make that has not previously been made." When we extent our hearts and minds and take an uncomfortable step to go beyond ourselves for the benefit of others, that is when healing energies become enabled; these positive energies can and do change the earth in so many harmonious ways. There is "nothing you can know that isn't known." The message is the same, only it is changed in new and creative ways to help and assist you to move positively forward along your various paths.

Close your eyes and in your own way enter into your own meditative state, your place of peace and safety. Soar with me as a barn swallow, rising swiftly into the sky to greet the sun at the dawn of day. Fly with me over the Rio Grande, through the canyons, over the rocks, through the trees. As a barn swallow, this is my world, my perspective. I arrive back at my nest and sing my energetic song. We must give each other the freedom to play and be as a child—innocent, energetic, and untouched in the continual astounding beauty of daily life, all the qualities and graces of being human. These are the moments that touch the heart and soul of the Universe, never to be forgotten, cherished and the perfected embodiment of Aries.

There on a distant peak, unseen by physical senses, an angel sings forth a triumphant note across the mountains and planes. In the distant seas, far away, the waves hear the magical note and greet its confirmation with joy, as the newness of waves greet the rocks on shore: all is well, all is whole, and all is one in joy, peace, and wellness of being.

Across the earth, another angel sings forth another empowering force from atop the highest peak amid winds and weather, and it moves fast across the face of the planet: Indeed, it is true all you need is love.

In your own way, come back to this room, but remember, you are all the empowerment of truth and love.

Aries is ruled by Mars and is the exaltation of the sun, the detriment of Venus, the home of Mars, the fall of Saturn, the harmony of Pluto, and the inharmony of Uranus. Aries is a cardinal and fire sign. Aries lives in the present. Aries is aggressive, nervy, fiery, quick, eager, impulsive, competitive, courageous, sympathetic, honest, dynamic, creative, and enthusiastic. Aries is a born leader, a pioneer, and an initiator of things. Aries, in their world, always comes first and sees everything from a "me first" perspective. Aries on the downside is often intolerant, quick-tempered, violent, temperamental, bitter, piercing, blunt, and hurtful and can lack follow-through. Aries likes to tell it like it is, often landing into hot water with other people. Others may see Aries as being selfish at times.

Major Arcanum XIII: The Reaper: Remember, then, sons and daughters of the earth, that terrestrial things are of short duration and that the highest powers are reaped as the grass of the field through the powers of truth and love via daily life. If Arcanum XIII should appear in the prophetic signs of your horoscope, the dissolution of your organs will come sooner than you might expect, but know that you are so much more than your mere physical existence. Remember, do not dread your physical demise, for death is but the step forward toward another and more glorious life. The Universe reabsorbs without ceasing all that springs from her bosom that has not spiritualized itself. But the releasing of ourselves from material instincts by a free and voluntary adhesion of our souls to the laws of universal movement constitutes in us the creation of a second being, a celestial soul, and begins our immortality. Seize the day!

We would encourage you to read Spiritual Astrology, our Course 7, where you can find Aries has been given the key phrase: I am.

> There is no death! What seems so is transition:
> This life of mortal breath
> Is but a suburb of the life Elysian
> Whose portal we call death.

Chapter Six

Understanding the Challenge and Beauty of Being Human

"What would you do if I sing out of tune? Would you turn and walk out on me?"

We are here to talk about all the goodness, graces, and blessings there are about being human—very much a Virgo thing, even if you don't think so! In the sacredness, we are very much here to embrace all the dignity, all the passion, all the unending bliss surrounding all the relationships between the Universe and the people—all the people, including each of you!

At the same time, I stand before you to say that intelligence is not all that it's cracked up to be! There is that part about human interaction that absolutely makes no sense at all! But in fact, it is that very human interaction that brings out the very best qualities and virtues of being Virgo.

Virgo is ruled by Mercury and is the inharmony of the moon, the home of Mercury, the fall of Venus, the detriment of Jupiter, the harmony of Saturn, and the detriment of Neptune. Virgo is classified an earth, mutable, summer, nocturnal, dry, and feminine sign. Virgo qualities are the following: virtuous, chaste, barren, common, mental, humane, talkative, unfortunate, critical, analytical, picky, fussy, detailed, methodical, faultfinding, intolerant of the views and opinions of others, selfish, receptive, susceptible, unsympathetic, and weakened by fear and adverse suggestions, and they should think in terms of health rather than disease.

Life can be really crappy sometimes, as we all know. Virgo people can often end up with their backs to the wall with seemingly nowhere to go or nowhere to turn. What do you do? Do you analyze your way out of it? Do you wait it out, ignore it, and hope it goes away? Do you face it head-on, conquer, or be conquered? Or do you turn tail, run, and hope it does not follow you? Well, Virgo has found ways to do those things and more, but do it in such more positive and methodical ways!

Now the Church of Light does not teach this, but this is what I personally think. I believe that some of us are here on this planet today from the future, having incarnated from the future into the past in order to heal, make whole, and bring various situations into oneness again; to respond in ways now that manifest greater harmony; and to remind ourselves and souls of others who we really are. Therefore, I must point out that there is a Higher Mind with whom we are all connected and that is who we really are. It is this Higher Mind within each of us that realizes the graces and blessings of being human in continually unique and live fulfilling events yet to be profoundly realized.

Given the opportunity in our daily lives, when the world pauses and in some way personally reaches out to us, we must extend hope to every soul we can, both human and animal. When others reach out to us, we must take the time to be with each other and make a difference toward hope and enlightenment. Given the proper nourishment, the soul can recover, grow, and blossom to make our earth a better place—again all the qualities, dignity, and blessings of being human.

Veiled Isis-Arcanum II: Remember then, sons and daughters of the earth, that the mind is enlightened in seeking God with the eyes of the will. God had said, "Let there be light," and light inundated space. Man should say, "Let truth show itself and good come to me." And if man possesses a healthy will, he will see the truth shine, and guided by it, he will attain all that he aspires. If veiled Isis should appear in the prophetic signs of your horoscope, strike resolutely at the door of the future and it will open to you, but study for a long time the door

29

you should enter. Turn your face toward the sun of justice, and the knowledge of the true will manifest in your very being. Keep silent with regard to your intentions so as not to be influenced by the contradictions continuing around you.

My wife Radine's father is Ray Hayes, deceased, born September 6, 1932, Virgo sun sign. From our Course 11, Divination and Character Reading, we know that good powers of reflection, sound judgment, and intelligence are indicated from a temple that is wide above the forehead and by the length from the head to the ears forward. That is Ray.

Ray had a difficult life, with his back to the wall a number of times, as many of us have had or will have! With Jupiter in the cusp in the seventh house, he had multiple marriages, not all harmonious. But Ray, like all of us, rose to the occasion and made the best out of it that he could, not to the liking or acceptance of many: such is the power of love, the paths of which are not always so easy. Does Virgo make mistakes? Well yes, but at the end of the day, the real question is, do we learn from the mistakes that we all make in life? To those of you who would be judgmental of Virgo, I would say this: let it go. Embrace instead the greater cosmic love!

Because as the Beatles said: "All we need is a little help from our friends. All we need is a little help from our friends. We need each other. We need each other to love."

Let us close our eyes and tune our senses away from the outside world. In your own way, enter into your own space on the inter plane.

Out of the darkness a single beam of light shines forth. This is the special glow of your soul showing your path forward diffusing into multiple colors.

Unique sounds accompany your beam. You manifest into the physical amid many beams of light, each different. At the same time, some beams of light are leaving to transform to other planes.

There comes the first breathe as you cry out, entering through a doorway of pain and suffering, but with a promise of greater things to come.

Date, time and place are noted to create your natal chart, a map of your soul, all the energies you brought with you up to that moment.

Across the earth, an angel sings forth an empowering acknowledging force from atop the highest peak, amid winds and imponderable weather; it moves rapidly across the face of the earth to embody and transform all in its path. It is true; like waves washing ashore henceforth, now, and forever, all you need is love.

Chapter Seven

Bringing an End to Nincompoopism: The Reinforcement and Cosmic Supporting of the Human Soul

The Universe informed me recently that only one-tenth of 1 percent gets up in the middle of the night to interact when called upon. Really, of all the population on this planet, only one-tenth of 1 percent is awake enough to interact with all that is, was, or will ever be? I find that hard to believe. What do you say to the Universe? "Not now, I'm sleeping." "You're a figment of my imagination; not real!" Wake up, people! Be open to having your unique interaction with the Universe, unique to this planet. Despite all the hardships of your present life, there is a higher priority that you must respond to. It takes rising above yourself in order to respond, interact, and play with the Universe. Well, I can tell you this; I don't want to be that one-tenth of 1 percent! I want everyone else to be there too. Please be awake to the needs of the Universe. I can definitely say this; these interactions spark infinite worth and overwhelming satisfaction often down sometimes difficult paths, but in the end, you shall never regret it!

Perhaps my friend from abroad is right, "The world is overrun with nincompoopism," a new word, perhaps! It seems every day we run into yet another jackass that botches it up rather badly. The only thing we can do is to pause, stare into their beady eyes, and say, "Please try again!"

Let us arise to the occasion and definitely not give up on humanity, for the nincompoop of today can one day grow to become the sage of tomorrow. This I believe.

I had originally composed this sermon to give you a view into the lives of my mother and father, both Capricorns, both born January 9, different years, and my sisters and family life, but as time moved on, my mother, from the inner plane, objected to sharing such personal information. So as to guard each soul's dignity and pride, I have removed it. I guess Capricorn is a bit secretive too, as is Scorpio, being me. I ask you, when censored, what is there left to talk about other than what is currently present in our daily lives?

Gemini the cat was so named because he arrived at our Burbank home slightly after Sylvester did back in 2002. They were obvious brothers, looking alike, both gray and white, but as both alpha males at the time, Gemini was intent on killing Sylvester, an obvious Mars thing! Sylvester did not move as fast as Gemini; he was more like the godfather kitty— demanding respect, kiss the paw, but if Sylvester did manage to catch you, he would clamp his teeth on to your hand until you figured a way out, often distracting him with the other free hand, offering it as bait, but withdrawing it just in time, only to free the other hand. Eventually, Gemini and Sylvester arrived at a tolerant coexistence, with only an occasional spat—only if our earth could do that!

We are born with our sun sign, but in actuality we seemingly do embody all twelve signs from time to time. Such is the case with Gemini the cat. Sometimes, he is a Pisces—dreamy, flighty, and altruistic. He had for most of his life one of those progressed Jupiter aspects to the sixth house and/or first house: i.e., fat! I feed all the cats when I arise at 2:30 a.m., unless Radine, my wife, in a manic state, beats me too it, often not to my liking. If I try to sleep in, they begin a kitty protest until I do get up and feed them, seven cats plotting, now six. About 5:00 a.m. as I prepare for my daily exercise, I move Cuddles, the Taurus cat, who has an eating disorder—binge eating; he would keep eating dry food all day. He sits near the kitchen table all day, dozing on a nearby chair, but as soon as cat food is presented to another hungry cat, there Cuddles appears. Prior to my morning exercise, I confine Cuddles to the sunroom and lock the door, while the remaining cats enjoy dry food for a brief time in the kitchen.

Cuddles, a Taurus earth sign, will probably make a nice Sumo wrestler in a future human incarnation. Or Cuddles, being black and white, would make an interesting killer whale. Radine one day brought home a sample of dry food, but Cuddles ate it all at once. He ended up at our vet for a week and we almost lost him. We were glad he decided to stay.

Gemini, of course during that time, tried for some time to have crunches as well, but as time moved on, his body could not tolerate the dry food. He was fourteen or fifteen at the time with only ten out of thirty cat teeth left. You see, even cats have teeth problems. At the beginning of August 2013, a once Gordo cat, Gemini had lost two-thirds of his body weight, quite a physical difference! Still the alpha male, he was in charge, and if the front door opened even slightly, we could move like lightning before you could say otherwise, out the door. (And my words, "You damn cat, get back here," were in vain! It was not always safe out there in the real world.) His escape was an annoyance perhaps, but also something to silently admire as well, gumption!

About 7:00 a.m., I stopped to empty the trash with Ms. Dog, Elsa, our golden retriever. I put away the cat's dry food and released Cuddles from the sunroom. I always left Cuddles a few of each type of the three various dry crunches on the table, and if he was fast enough, he got to eat those before another cat did.

Gemini, as the alpha male, blamed me for his weight loss. It was my fault, as I was not feeding him enough. He would get behind my chair while I was working and stare at me in disgust. He would run between my legs while I was seated at my desk, until I would get up and feed him. And then if I moved to the bathroom down our hallway, when I emerged, there would be Gemini staring at me and meowing at the top of his lungs for more food. He became quite the bitchy cat in his old age, but in the night he would curl up at the foot of my waterbed where I slept and slowly worked his way up to me to be held. Such is the power of love! On more than one occasion, I would awake to find him on my waterbed headboard above me and staring my way, only to sneeze all over me. (If you haven't guessed, this uses some of the energy of my progressed aspects to my sixth house, ruling small pets. Thank goodness, he is not a horse with an aspect to my twelfth house, where I would be trampled upon!)

Gemini's belly no longer moves from side to side as he runs down the hallway, as it once did. And Elsa the dog no longer helps me to empty the trash in the morning; it was no longer a new endeavor. At the end of the day, after all the trials and errors, I love them all: the pets and all the family members we daily interacted with, but who do not wish to share their intimate secrets; such is life and its profound intimacy! But it is those special interactions we have with family members in our daily lives, even if, at times, we did not even realize it was a special moment at the time, but both for better or worse create in us the realizations of the Kingdoms of Heaven's immeasurable value and worth!

Every kid needs someone to lean on, even if at the time you did not think you needed it. Kids by themselves think they can take on the world, but they are wrong, even if they do not realize or want to admit it at the time. My dad passed away when I was seven going on eight in a head-on collision, auto accident. For as long as I remember, everyone in my life looked to me for strength, support, and fortitude. Maybe I share these true animal soul stories because it reminds me so much of my life in ways. Who do you think I leaned on as a child of seven going on eight and for all the years to come? I give you one guess: it was and is the Universe. Well, by the grace of the Universe, I did not know it at the time.

On August 18, 2016, about 3:00 p.m. Gemini passed on to the next life. I knew he was not doing so good. I fed him every time he asked. He gave out a cry in our hallway such as I have not heard in some time.

We all stopped what we were doing and went to him. Yes, it was a doorway of pain and suffering, but truly with a promise of a better life yet to come. I chose to bless Gemini on his path forward, having observed in his soul steadfastness, determination, leadership, resoluteness, persistence, and success, and absolutely yes, with all my heart, I love you on your way forth.

Capricorn is ruled by Saturn and is the detriment of the moon, the exaltation of Mars, the fall of Jupiter, the home of Saturn, and the inharmony of Neptune. Capricorn is classified as an earth, cardinal, changeable, winter, unfortunate, and feminine sign. This sign is ambitious, cautious, materialistic, practical, cold, indifferent, efficient, intelligent, responsible, perfectionist, hardworking, uses others to get ahead, stingy, egotistical, negative, nocturnal, domestic, traditional, and hurtful and has weak vitality, good business sense, and serious sense of humor. (I love Capricorn because I know it so well.) Due to illnesses, Capricorns need to move to strengthen vitality and guard against despondence and melancholy to stay well and balanced.

The Balance—Major Arcanum VIII: Remember then, sons and daughters of the earth, that to be victorious over yourself and dominate obstacles is but a part of your human task. To accomplish it entirely, you must establish equilibrium between the forces that are continually present in your daily life. All actions produce reactions. The will should foresee the shock of opposite forces in order to temper or annul them. If the balance should appear in the prophetic signs of your horoscope, it signifies that the future is balanced between good and evil and warns that an unbalanced mind is like an abortive sun.

I wrote a book years ago, *People of Passion: Journeys in Heavens of Heaven*. I was never able to get it published, but today I thought it appropriate, as we approach the winter solstice, to share with you the final chapter, as a meditation of sorts. (By the way, my wife Radine said I could probably get it published, if I had a sensual cover! Passion—indeed, it is a word open to various understandings, as if the love of the Universe does not rate these days!) I will also share with you this: The Universe, the Cosmic Mind, from a time I was young would wake me up late at night, as now, and ask me to rewrite this work. I feel a universal love from this endeavor—a spark, an emotional hug, which if we accomplished this work, we could change the earth and make it a better place for all souls. An ambitious dream perhaps, but not so, says the Universe, a task to which I was born. At first, I thought, "Well, let's perfect this and make it better." But then by the twenty-fifth rewrite or so, as editors go, I began to understand that this was also a way for the Universe to feel love, support, and nourishment, but at the same time, it had unique sparks of truths to it, a give-and-take of unique and empowering love toward positive change. (Everyone calls upon God, the Universe, for love and support, but who can the Universe call upon other than you or someone else who might have the innate desire to respond in kind and be open to unique interactions?) I came to embrace a loving energy who had to, moment to moment, day to day, tried unceasingly to respond to unbalanced souls, many who are insane and who need to find ways back to something better from an unbalanced existence. We (the Universe and I) continued to rewrite, edit, and find better paths toward a more harmonious and supportive future for all the human souls. (It stems from an internal cosmic desire that there has to be solutions for all souls; we are all born for specific purposes, that we have to go forward and never give up, until we can embrace all souls in oneness and cosmic love together.) After various rewrites, more than I can count or an editor could transform, at the end of this endeavor, the following is the final chapter for *People of Passion: Journeys in the Kingdoms of Heaven*—maybe. (Keep in mind that these words have multiple meanings, encouragement, and strength, beyond various understandings, open to various understandings. These scenes are products of our own times, but should I say, the depths of realization have yet to come.)

Close your eyes and in your own way go into your place of peace, oneness, and meditation.

The Eternal Love of God

The captain is preparing the ship for takeoff from the planet earth. Stars in the night from distant worlds reflect in the captain's eyes, like new dreams yet to discover and enjoy.

Alome and I are contentedly cuddling together on a nearby sofa. The light is dim, like a romantic and warm glow that would be made from loving human hearts.

The captain is talking with us.

"I like to share a lifetime within each person," the captain begins.

"I have felt both of you develop from within me. In my silent love, my presence from within you grew and actualized in your uniqueness. You discovered it is actually I who am within you. I do not reveal myself because I want each soul to find me within their own hearts and thus enter and discover the Kingdoms of Heaven, which is my presence interacting within each soul."

"We are present to each other," Alome says, hugging Etlov's arm.

"But this is only the beginning of the Kingdoms of Heaven unraveling before you. Our unity and love knows no limitation.

"I am going to take my leave of you and return to my planet. From there I will continue to enjoy, feel, and interact with the vast creation.

"Etlov, you were right when we first met. I am the Universe or God in a form you can relate with. We shall never be apart. My heart and truth continually go out to encounter each soul, as I have with both of you. I shall never forget you. I am the captain, but you are both unique captains of your own heart, mind, and soul.

"Your names, as you now remember them, represent your special blessings for your lives on the earth. Your names have special graces forever. Etlov means eternal love. And Alome means alpha and omega. In your unity, my presence of eternal love always was and will always be.

"As we now part our company, the two of you will now go forth toward universal cosmic structures yet to be embraced. There are many souls for you both to encounter forever and ever. May you take your blessings to them and may they bring their blessings to you."

As Etlov and Alome embrace while listening to his words, the captain disappears from their sight, but never very far from their hearts.

◆ ◆ ◆

We are once again back in the gothic theater, each of us resting in our plush theater seats. The director again appears on stage, along with his wife, looking a little tired from a night of dancing.

"The many that became as one may now go forth as individuals again into the night. Become aware, however, that this work continues on in your own life, wherever you go. This story never ends. It continues forever in every person's heart. This story is your story and shall continue forever as you discover your Kingdoms of Heaven within each of you.

"The future stories of your lives will foretell that the presence of the Universe within your hearts and souls permanently dwells therein.

"And that you might not go forth from this theater sad, lonely, per-plexed, or in any other state of consciousness other than joyous, consider the following before departing, once again as one."

◆ ◆ ◆

Two children are at play outside a city church. It is Saturday. They see an elderly custodian is just about finished cleaning the church for the next day Sunday service. They watch him go out to the back to wash and clean a bucket of mop water.

"Now's the time," he says to her.

"I don't know. I want to, but I'm afraid."

He is about twelve with dark hair and she is nine with reddish blond hair.

He begins skipping toward the church in his playful and innocent nature.

"Come on," he shouts to her.

She lets him get almost to the church and then in a fast sprint joins him.

The elderly custodian in the back of the church is washing out the mop in the bucket, when all of a sudden he hears the church bells ringing. He puts down the mop and hurriedly makes his way to the front of the church.

There on two of the three bell ropes are the children bouncing up and down, giggling with delight.

"You two children, stop that," the custodian shouts.

"Oh, come on and join us," shouts back the young boy.

The custodian pauses, thinks a moment, and then runs to the empty bell rope.

"You know, I've always wanted to do this," he says, ringing the bell with delight.

Chapter Eight

Elvis, the Mischievous Cat!

Elvis, a small and tiny black cat, showed up at our Burbank home one day out of the blue. Maybe that should have been a warning to me. My wife, Radine, took to Elvis and she wanted to keep that cat. Elvis, at that time unnamed, had a tag on him with a phone number that Radine called. It was a number of a local pet shop that had lost a black cat in our neighborhood. Radine, kindhearted as she is, took the cat back to the pet shop. It turned out he was for sale, for one hundred dollars. Well, one hundred dollars later, we had in our hands Elvis the cat.

He looked so feminine that I thought for sure he was a female. I said to Radine, "Get this cat to our vet and get her fixed before she has kittens." Our vet took one look at this cat and said, "No charge, neutered male," with a laugh. That should have been a clue. But not everything is as it seems. It is best to not make conclusions or judgment based on appearances alone.

That was years ago, in Burbank, and here we are today in Albuquerque, New Mexico, having lived here for ten years now. We moved here in a historic snowstorm in the beginning of winter 2016. It has now just turned 2017.

I used to sell waterbeds at eighteen, Creative Bedding, in Oxnard, California. And so did my sister, Celeste; she recommended me for that job. I still like waterbeds, as you can have a four-drawer foundation beneath your waterbed where you can store various clothing. I like neatness, orderliness, structure, and a home well organized. Radine is a clutter-type person and tries to avoid throwing anything away. I like to keep things in a certain place so I know where it is. My wife, Radine, only on occasion, places things back where it originally was. I am used to this now and just look around until I find it. Then comes Elvis into the room, who, while I am out of the bedroom, opens each of the four drawers and throws my underwear, socks, handkerchiefs, and other clothing high into the air onto the floor and rolls in delight with them. Then, as I pause in my work, here I come to discover this disaster.

Then comes Mr. Hound, also from Burbank, who thinks he is a dog, but is really a cat, because he was raised with baby dogs and does not relate too well with cats. Our other cats here in Albuquerque pick on him because he does not fit in. The end result is the other cats pick on him so much that he is afraid to use the litter box. Therefore, he pees and poos in the kitchen and living room. I am not so fond of cleaning this up, to say the least, but I have to remind myself that I am a forgiving and compassionate soul, not so easy sometimes.

In my bedroom, I have a sliding-mirror closet that can open in four ways. There is a middle shelf for various clothing. On either side of the middle shelf are both a higher rack for clothes and a lower rack for clothes. On the lift, quite high, are hooks for clothes. They are so high that I think they were perhaps put there to hang vestments, as the previous owner was a priest for the Eastern Orthodox.

I kept this closet closed to protect my clothing. But in the distant past, there comes Elvis and opens the closet to expose my clothing. Mr. Hound decides to go to that one safe area where no one could see him peeing, raises his tail, and sprays my clothing on the lower racks to his heart's content; of course, I remind myself that it is nothing that a fresh wash could not fix. Since then, I have used various weights to keep the closet closed. So far, so good!

My conclusion finally is that order and having everything organized and in a specific place may be a good idea and my preferable way, but at the end of the day it is not that big a deal, especially when it comes to other people and pets that we love. I must admit that a part of me quivers at it, but really, what are a few messes, after all? One day, there is the ideal, but today it is more important to advance consciousness on our world, and that is the main focus.

I remember one morning awakening to move toward the kitchen to get a cup of coffee. There was Elvis in Radine's arms on the living room couch, receiving love. We must embrace and empower love, wherever it is.

Then, as a saving grace, there is Sancho, a neighborhood dog, a very large and white pit bull. The first time I encountered him in our yard, he was so large I had goose bumps on my arms. This was a dog who could do significant damage, if he wanted. It turned out he was a lover and not an aggressive dog. He would just prefer to lick you rather than bite you. But if you did not know, at that time he posed an ominous threat. I gave Sancho a few dog treats, a hug, and sent him on his way, or so I thought.

It turned out that Sancho was quite the escape artist. There did not seem to be a fence that could keep him in. Quite frequently, in the summer of 2016, I would awake at my usual 2:30 a.m. time to find him whimpering or asleep at our front door. Well, my heart went out to him, and I gave him more treats and hugs, along with a small bed to lie on.

At a decent hour or so, I would then call our neighbor Amanda to come and collect Sancho. She would show up in her truck. Other times, her son would show up, and then Sancho would get into the truck and go back home again.

When I would walk Elsa, our golden retriever, later in the day, we would sometimes pass by Sancho's home, and there he would be at the fence to greet us, always hopeful for a biscuit or something, always given with joy.

One recent evening when I was in a dream state, I was playing a sort of basketball with folks from a Higher Minded club, an astral plane experience. Let it be known, I am not an athletic person, by any means, to which my wife can confirm. But here I was playing basketball. And I moved and blocked this other person's shot. Then someone looked into my eyes and threw me the ball. I turned and shot and the ball almost hung there in midair, falling in toward the basket. It was a narrow basket, not your standard.

Then others on the opposing team were able to cast some magical spell to prevent the ball from dropping in. There were sparks of blue and white light beneath the rim. Then I extended my hands and, without touching the ball, willed the ball through. Apparently, that was it, and the game was over. I was now a member of the club and accepted in.

Then came two large cats, almost human-like, to be present. One cat was an extremely large orange cat, but with long blond hair. The cat stretched its body and quivered as it shook its long blond hair into place and wiggled its body along into harmonic satisfaction of movement. It was satisfying and empowering to behold. You could feel such satisfaction in the movement of this cat that it was healing and satisfying. Now in waking life, when I pet our orange cat, Junior, I think of this cat and feel a similar energy of satisfaction, a stretching and an embrace of life. But this was a cat on the astral plane that was preparing to advance into a human incarnation. A future blond, I would guess, male or female, to be determined. After all, everyone can have long blond hair these days!

The Universe is never outdone in generosity. Perhaps that was my saving grace in my life. For one day, I found myself moving along the water's path near our home in Albuquerque, a dream, perhaps. As I began this journey from our home, I could hear the local dog alarms from the neighborhood dogs sounding around us. As I began my walk with Elsa, one by one, various dogs from the neighborhood somehow escaped and joined us along the path. I woke up, but remembered that there I was, walking with hundreds of dogs, all in delight. Such is the power of love! What begins as a sacrifice and then turns into an act of kindness and giving can and does result in bliss. Moments of sacrifice when reflected upon years later can be sources of triumph and great joy, something of unlimited worth.

I remember as a small child I used to fall asleep in my backyard in the summer under the stars, asleep in a backyard recliner. My sister, Celeste, would carry me into our home and place me in my bed. We shared a bedroom; she was about ten years older than me. I was probably five or six years old at the time, she fifteen or sixteen.

We would dream together and we would fly. Others would try to hold us back, but we could rise above them. Off we would go into the sky, moving forward to save the world. Maybe I watched too many Superman episodes as a child, but the flying experiences were real, at least when I was asleep. Of course, as you grow up, you realize you cannot fly anymore. But there is that part of me that when I now drift off to sleep, walking with our many dogs along water's paths, that thinks I can indeed still fly and no one can stop me or hold me back. And a real part of me believes, knows, so can the rest of our world.

One evening when I was asleep, I was with Radine on the inner plane in the city. It is a fairly large city with many steep steps. I remember passing by a bookstore and peeking in the front door; there were so many books stacked to the ceiling, row after row after row. I was tempted to go in, but I had something more pressing to accomplish.

Dr. Masters seems to have a place here. I have had several experiences with him here since his passing in 2016. He has his own place on the inner plane (Dr. Paul Leon Masters, founder of the University of Metaphysics). He is a good soul; he worked hard and genuinely to heal our earth while alive. He sent me across town with Radine, my wife, to give a talk on that very subject.

Radine was driving me, something that does not usually happen on the real planet earth! I turned to her and said, "I left without my notes. I would feel more comfortable with my notes to give a talk concerning ways to create ceremonial magic to heal the earth."

Radine said to just speak from my experiences. "You don't need notes."

We arrived at this place that was full of people, some I knew. There was my junior high school English teacher, Mrs. Kess. Before I knew her as that, I first met her in the park as a child while she was walking her dog. We had a number of good conversations then, when I was in first grade, but at that time, I used to run away from school and go to the small local park. I used to get picked on in first grade; others would act up, and when the teacher turned around, everyone would look at me. So I would escape to the park. That was probably one of the reasons I flunked first grade, but maybe it was a good start to something better down the road.

Everyone seemed happy to see me there. Mrs. Kess had a very long and protruding nose. People greeted her by affectionately holding her nose. I did the same when she passed by, and she said, "An affectionate hello, I am sure." Memories fade over the years, and what seemed so important at the moment, in fact, ultimately gives way to greater things. Every day when I get up, I begin my day by asking, "How can we make this earth a better place? How can we heal the earth?" I assumed at the time that everyone else was doing and asking the same; that is, my Neptune influence in my fourth house of the home also may be a good thing. Then, after that, I have to face the realities of my life and take care of what I had to.

The requirements to perform ceremonial magic include having a large group of people gathered together for a specific purpose, being it a lecture, talk, healing ceremony, conference, or something along these lines. Then you give a talk that evokes within them higher emotions of love, affection, reflection, comfort, joy, affection, longing for the greater good, kindness, and the attributes of the Higher Mind or God, the purposes for which each of these souls have incarnated into this human incarnation, but maybe not even realizing it at the time. But the Higher Mind realizes it constantly and each person's soul also realizes it constantly at some level, this reality not always manifesting into the physical plane, possibly because of the so many distractions we have in the physical plane.

This story evokes, reminds of hope in each individual soul in order to heal, and changes people's heart for the better. The next step in ceremonial magic is to summon or invite advance souls moving about the Universe to gather in your surroundings to empower specific healing. Healing begins emotionally on the soul level, but when empowered, energized, loved, warmed, given strength and grace, hugged, and enlightened, the best of life itself in all its goodness and kindness can change circumstances for the better. Once empowered, these electric energies find its various ways and paths to manifest into the physical plane and to heal according to the needs of the individual. What actually heals is not the one leading the ceremony, but it is the power of the Universe.

Then someone, while I was sharing this, in the room turned to me and said, "Well, Patrick, you are an advanced soul." That stopped me because I never considered myself as that. We are born here and we do not know our history once we have incarnated here. We forget our past, and rightly so. Whether we are an advanced soul or not does not matter for this incarnation. What matters is that we give our utmost. The only thing that really matters is that we heal the earth.

Healing energy can often work over time. The lecture may have ended, but the healing goes forth well into the future. What you do today to heal, support, love, and provide comfort can have profound manifestation in ways you may never know, but one day will. Then too there are souls whom I so wanted show up for the lecture, but were absent. In so many ways, that's what keeps me up at night sometimes. I want them to know how much they are loved. Some insecure part of me clings to and believes that these healing energies do ultimately reach their soul across all barriers, earthly or self-imposed because such is the power of love, a love once again that knows no bounds across time or space.

We have walked into the desert together, wilderness of sorts, with a large body of people. It is warm, perhaps summer. There is lightning and thunder in the distance, moving our way. I raise my arms over the masses, "Be healed, and with that confident power, make the earth whole again." The distant storm arrives and showers us with waters. The lightning and thunder dissipate and give way to the sun amid rainbows, giving hope for greater things to come. Many times, after working with the Universe to compose these very writings, I retire to the living room with a glass of wine to relax, prop up my feet on a footstool, and further commune with the Universe and other souls in relaxation and oneness. On these occasions, I am often surrounded by choirs, many angels and souls gathered together singing.

Tonight, I viewed so many choirs, one rapidly after another, some small and some large. Some make mistakes and the director just explodes, especially at rehearsal. We all make mistakes, but what I want you to know is the Universe does not see your mistakes, but instead sees your heartfelt love for what you are singing, your expression of love. At the end of a rather hard day of work, that is what makes the Universe's day, that heartfelt love. A special thank-you goes to you, an artist, perfect or not!

You may not realize this at the time, but with you is another choir in the backdrop. One day then, a curtain would slowly draw forth to reveal millions of choir members standing behind you. At first it would be silent, followed by brilliance, going beyond any expression of possible words. One day, you too will be part of this choir as well as your director. Together you will make such music!

Chapter Nine

The Story of Being Human

There is often nothing more comforting or relaxing, for that matter, than listening to a dog drinking water. Here I am working away at my computer when, out of the blue, lap, lap, lap, lap, and it continues for several minutes. Sometimes, I speak out, "Thirsty dog!" Other times, I just listen and relax in the sound; it is the genuine appreciation of water, something many just take for granted, but listening to the dog drinking water, you realize what a blessing it truly is.

Then a few minutes later, here comes the dog, smiling ear to ear, and gives my leg a juicy lick. The first few times it happened, I was not so pleased, but then I began to realize it was a sharing of a blessing, a cleansing, a healing of sorts, an expression of love.

That brings us then to an appreciation of human life. What causes us or brings us to incarnate into human life? There is the cycle of necessity. What we teach in the Church of Light is that the soul moves from celestial to spiritual to astral to mineral to vegetable to animal to human to astral to spiritual, and then once again to celestial. When we are on this path, the soul divides into two, male and female, till one day when they reunite as soul mates, having the richness of experiencing various physical incarnations separately, but later as one.

The Universe can and does move beyond this to fulfil, resolve, and respond to the various many needs of the present moment on a specific planet. Yes, incarnations can and do occur on numerous planets. Then there is the individual soul that reaches out and responds to an earnest and heartfelt prayer, having already gone through the various cycles of necessity. But as it turns out, necessity dictates a greater path to empower, support, love, and heal. I wonder, does the soul mate also reincarnate for the same purpose? A call to perfect, move forth, strengthen, and endure? I do not know for sure, but I trust in the Universe.

This was my foundation for incarnating into this life, an earnest response to a heartfelt prayer by a human being. Maybe it was a mistake, but as soon as I say that, I know it was not because of the many blessings that manifested because of it.

My father, Thomas Clayton Ramsey, born January 9, 1921, Springfield, Ohio, at 10:25 p.m. was in my mother's bedroom, Patricia Agnes Ramsey, born January 9, 1913, Pittsburg, Kansas, at 12:00 a.m. He told my mother that she would not get pregnant if he rubbed this on himself before sex. It turned out that it was shoe polish! This is the story of my conception that my mother later shared with me.

My father was a navy man with a dry sense of humor. He served on a ship, like many in World War II. He died when I was eight due to a head-on collision while coming back to Burbank from Arizona. He was strict, but kind. As a child, I had a black cat named Tuffy. I remember my father looking at that cat and saying, "Now don't you scratch him."

I remember going on a trip to the Santa Monica beach with him, my mother, and my sister, Celeste. I was too young to swim, but he took me out well beyond the breakers. I remember a whale swimming nearby. My father said, "Now you don't need to be afraid. This whale is your friend."

I remember going on a car ride to see his mother, and he heard the tire starting to leak. He pulled over, and sure enough, the car had a front flat. A nearby gas station helped fix that. In the meantime, there was a nearby park and he pushed me on a swing.

Aunt Marie, my father's sister, one Saturday showed up with her two sons at our house there in Burbank with a new red bicycle for me, but she was crying. She was the one who told my mother of my father's passing.

Many years later and after my mom had passed on, Marie showed up during a Mass at St. Finbar Catholic Church in Burbank. I was a Eucharist minister at that time, and in the back of the church it was the first time she had seen me in many years. I presented the Host to her and proclaimed, "The Body of Christ." It was not until that moment, when I looked into her eyes, did I even realize how much I had grown and how very much I looked like my father. She passed away not too long after that before we could have a good chat. What occurs to me now, as incarnations go, is that indeed how much each of us truly is the incarnation of the Cosmic Mind, moving on various purposeful paths.

I have to be careful here and not share too many intimate things. I have already decided to protect both the dignity and pride of my parents, as they are still a real part of my physical life, emotionally attached to me and now on the inner plane. Yet what is there to be afraid of? I say that, but yet immediately there is that fear. I will respect that and share what is possible. You see, some things can only be worked out and resolved on the inner plane. You think perhaps you have gotten away with something and no one will ever know; well, think again! You think you can pray your way to higher good through words alone and fool even the Universe; well, no you can't. If you think you can take, even slightly, advantage of others in order to get ahead in life, well, do not go there; you had best think again!

Certainly, we have all made mistakes in our lives. Sometimes we have botched it up rather badly. All of us have to face that one day. We have to look into the beady eyes of those we have offended and make amends so that all wounds are healed. So many fear this, but it is actually freeing, healing, and empowering. It enables you to move on with further strength and empowerment to do greater things into the future.

My mother, Patricia, a Capricorn, like my father, was strict. The key words for Capricorn are "I use." She was a loving and affectionate mother, very possessive. Every Saturday, I would dust and clean the house. Saturday night we would watch *The Dating Game*, *The Newlywed Game*, and *The Lawrence Welk Show*. Every Sunday morning, she would read me the Sunday funnies from the then *Herald Examiner*: Blondie and Dagwood, The Adventures of Prince Arthur. We would then go to the

12:15 p.m. Mass at St. Finbar, followed by grocery shopping at Vons. Capricorn thrives on routine and also for moments of quiet time of prayer and reflection.

As I grew, I became a newspaper boy for the *Independent* and then the *Burbank Daily Review* there in Burbank, California. I was able to contribute to the household from the paper route funds and start a small savings. I was shy and afraid to do the paper route in many ways. Every month, I would show up at the various households and hold up my collection receipts, "Hi, I am Pat and I'm collecting for the *Burbank Daily Review.*" That was me, at that time. In ways, even today, I am still that afraid, like a child, at the many ominous tasks we have at hand: a move from collecting money for a local newspaper to making ways to restore the earth, but a higher calling and strength moves me forward.

Then, as the years passed, I began to get to know these people I delivered newspapers to in a more intimate way, and my paper route, in many ways, evolved into a ministry, a give-and-take on a more heartfelt level, moments that I shall never forget and always cherish.

In the spring and summer, I would garden and plant vegetables. I planted tomatoes, squash, and sunflowers. Each year, I would count the number of tomatoes we had and tallied them on a kitchen easel. I would share the tomatoes with the neighbors and my paper route customers. There is nothing like the taste of fresh tomatoes!

My mother had planted a Valencia orange tree. I added a Navel orange tree in the front yard. Over the years, I added three different types of fig trees, an apple tree, and a Christmas tree in the backyard, along with various ferns. We had multiple rose bushes, annual bulbs that were there long before me, and large purple iris. Just taking care of the yard alone later became quite a weekly task, but a good one. I think perhaps I will still have this on the inner plane when I get there, even more expanded, although I have lost this for this part of my life.

Years earlier, my mother collected many rocks from various surroundings during her various travels in her old Nash; we had rock paths throughout our yard. I eventually had a cement walkway built around the backyard so she could walk around the yard and exercise and a hot tub to relieve her arthritis.

In the evening, my mom and I would play Canasta, Aggravation, Monopoly, and such. It was good, but what I did not have were friends of my own age, except at school, but as it turned out, that was not enough in the end. I made sacrifices to take care of family, as many do. I used to call her "my little buddy," and she was. We did have fun and love together.

My mother developed high blood pressure, mainly due to weight, in her sixties, passing away at seventy-five, January 13, 1988. She also had lymphoma at the time. It is odd what people actually pass away from. The medication they had her on for the lymphoma in turn lowered her immune systems. She caught a cold. She started having heart difficulties and ended up in the hospital. She had previously signed a "do not resituate" with her lymphoma doctor. She passed away from congestive heart failure in the hospital, not being resituated.

When she passed, and I was expecting to take her home from the hospital in a few days, our home seemed empty, vacant. Then there was so much to take care of, but I did manage to do it—the funeral, the burial, the mourning process. It was not until years later that I realized more about the death process, thanks to the Church of Light: Course 20, The Next Life, www.church.light

After death, each soul goes through a period of assimilation, a life review, and an incorporation of the various incarnations. For some people, it takes longer. With suicides, it takes even longer, but rest assured, no soul is ever lost. It was not until years later that I started having inner plane interactions with my mother. But when someone passes and you do not understand this at the time, there is such an emptiness, with the soul of this person no longer being around.

Years later, I understand it better and have since had inner plane communication with my mom. That being said, I have certainly given many of our pets' various send-off blessings when or before they passed and let them know how much I loved them. When my mom died, I used to write different things on our easel in the kitchen: "Treasures shall never be hidden beneath the sands of distant faraway island, but eternally present within our hearts." Today, therefore, Mother, here is my blessing to you: May the stability you so desire be always yours. May you be surrounded by and realize the wealth that is forever present within your own soul. May you bask in the tropical, spring-like surrounds, a much-needed break and vacation of sorts. And may you always know that I shall always love you.

Chapter Ten

Exploration in Astral Nature

In retrospect, life is a series of moments, some more intense than others, toward various paths of growth and development that continually evolves, develops, intensifies, and ultimately explodes in wonder across the cosmos onward toward greater adventure, creativity, wonder, and fulfillment.

In my place in the woods, there is a large fig tree, white type fig, growing unencumbered in the warm sun, in rich soil, unpruned and growing wild. It is at least fifty feet tall, draping its branches out in various directions, reaching its arms forth to embrace and bless its surrounds and the various forms of life around it. There, as large as your fist, is a ripe and juicy fig, oozing with juices like milk and honey as a fruit goes. It gives you joy, strength, and fulfilment to eat it. And in eating it, the tree, in fulfilling its purpose, experiences joy, strength, and fulfillment.

I offered my wife, Radine, this fig first, because to me it was so special, but she refused, finding the fig not to her liking. What is attractive to some is unattractive to others. Perhaps it is the packaging—not sure, but I sure enjoyed that fig.

On my various paths in the mountain trails, the mountain greets you with delight that you are there walking along its various paths. In the morning, the sun shines its various lights upon you to bask and glow as you follow various streams toward exploration and wonder at new discoveries. There are your various golden retrievers following you, often running ahead of you and then coming back in excitement to greet you, glad of your presence. They roll on their back, embracing some wondrous smell, a goodness that only a dog can recognize, the joys of life.

Mine is a place where you can plant many and various tomato plants, some pruned to perfection and others also growing unencumbered to see what will happen over time—an experiment. This is a place where you can taste the freshness of life and be satisfied, a place where you can love and be loved in freedom and goodness.

I was with Radine on a very high cliff, overlooking the vast sea, the ocean. I had a unique rock carving to be placed on a high pedestal overlooking the space between the land and the sea. This is a blessing to all present. But to place it on this pedestal, I had to cross a very narrow path in order to place it on its stand. The stand was about three feet round—thick, solid, and clear glass. I could look down, and it seemed like it was thousands of feet high, with rock and cliffs overlooking the sea waves crashing ashore below. Part of me knew I could fly, if need be, but I did not want to test it at the time. I placed this piece of blessing on its pedestal and slowly made my way back to land. It occurs to me that life is so much like that narrow path, whether you step one way or the other and off you go or not, because indeed we can fly.

We are born in this place, knowing we are eternal beings and that we can soar and fly in our freedom. Then, over time, we are slowly educated, well meaning, I'm sure. Constant rhetoric and lies can try to hold you back, but ultimately, I think it will necessarily fail because of the truth of our very nature. Goodness, kindness, and love shall always fly forth unencumbered.

Then one day we arrive at this place in the Universe that we can call home. It's our own place and others can visit and stay as needed and wanted. We have our own surroundings, books that we cherish. I love order and neatness, unlike my wife Radine, who attracts clutter. But I have to admit the clutter is interesting in a Cancer way—homely and comforting, at least to her. I have concluded that in in my life I have placed too much importance on order and neatness and not enough greater importance on living, something ultimately more important. We do learn various lessons from our physical lives!

I prefer to be surrounded by beauty, kindness, and love. I really don't like the other stuff. I can tolerate it for a time in an attempt to help others. This attempt is a greater path in itself because we have to leave and give up who and what we are to bless others and raise our consciousness to new levels of understanding and endeavor. We often do fail at these attempts, but when we succeed at times it is all worth it, without question.

It was one day in the past that one person discovered my true motive for doing what I was doing. He looked into my eyes and said, "What is more amazing is that you kept silent all this time and you were working to help me to arrive at a higher level of understanding." I did not catch this at first, but then I noticed one of my associates in this endeavor was crying. She was crying because she realized it was her motive too.

There is this higher calling beyond the place that we would normally call home. It is this higher calling that moves us forth way beyond our comfort zone in an attempt to help others. There are a number of us out there that get up each day, sometime in the middle of the night, to plot and plan ways forth to accomplish higher levels of understanding.

There is that part of me that thrives in my home with my plants and books, my various loves and thrills. At the same time, my soul necessarily responds and moves forth at the thought that someone is left behind. We simply cannot have that!

More to follow!

www.ingramcontent.com/pod-product-compliance
Lightning Source LLC
Chambersburg PA
CBHW060612030426
42337CB00018B/3053